CAULIFLOWER

Christopher Trotter

Photography by Caroline Trotter

For Jacques Eza,
an inspirational chef and good friend

© Christopher Trotter 2017

Published by Christopher Trotter.

A CIP catalogue record for this book is available from the British Library.

ISBN 978-0-9926830-5-4

Produced by Print & Design, University of St Andrews
Website: www.st-andrews.ac.uk/printanddesign

Printed by Latimer Trend & Company Limited

Distributed by Christopher Trotter
Tel: 07739049639

CONTENTS

INTRODUCTION

It took me a long time to get to like cauliflower. I still have a childhood memory of the smell of it cooking, and the fact that it was usually over-cooked for school lunches, my mental image is of a grey sludge with a gloopy cheese topping, sitting in a pool of water. Not a good start! Apparently, it is quite hard to grow so I don't remember it much from home-cooking as a child, as my mum grew most of our vegetables, so it has been a process of learning, mostly through cauliflower cheese, which Is typical student food; cheap and easy to prepare.

Dorothy Hartley in her book 'Food in England' (Macdonald and Co 1956) says that it is a Mediterranean plant. She recommends eating the outer leaves, claiming they are sweeter than cabbage, and suggests soaking in cold water for an hour before preparation to remove any 'lurking insects'! She liked to cook cauliflower whole and split the thick stem upwards a few times to speed up cooking.

However, in recent times, I have discovered how incredibly versatile a vegetable it is; equally happy with spices, as it is with fish and shell fish. It makes great soups and is lovely raw in salads. As Dorothy Hartley attests the outer leaves can be used as well and the stalk diced up and used as a garnish in soups or salads, maybe with a bit of quick cooking. Tips for avoiding the smell are to add a bay leaf to the water when cooking and cook it as quickly as possible. It appears that the smell is stronger the more it is cooked. I have also read that adding vinegar to the water helps, but this can mar the flavour in more delicate dishes.

VARIETIES AND SEASONS

Over the centuries varieties will have been improved and I cannot find much information about them. Common varieties appear to me to be more modern with names such as 'Galleon' and 'Snowball' showing their visual properties and then there are the colourful ones such as 'Romanesco', the striking green hybrid, or 'Di Sicilia Violetto' which is a beautiful purple colour.

Guy Watson from Riverford Farm says that cauliflowers are really cultivable all year round, but because of their need for nitrogen, are not at their best when over-wintered as they grow mushy, sappy and large. The best time, he says, for home-grown, organic cauliflowers is in the autumn and then again in April and May.

We are conditioned into looking for perfect white specimens, but do not be put off by slightly off-white or misshapen heads. Smaller, tighter grained caulis will have better flavour than their larger, looser counterparts. Try to buy them with the leaves still attached and not cling-wrapped in plastic. Cauliflowers will keep happily for a week or so in the fridge and having the leaves still attached is a sign of freshness.

NUTRITION

Cauliflower is a cruciferous vegetable, part of the Brassica family and thus is full of nutrients. Close to zero fat and sugar, it is high in Vitamin C, Vitamin A and Folates.

Recent research shows it is correlated with the prevention of chronic diseases such as cardiovascular diseases, diabetes, neurodegenerative disorders and various cancers.

Many of these nutrients can be destroyed by over-cooking, so light cooking will keep their nutrient content high and, as I have said earlier, will prevent the unpleasant smell that over- cooked cauliflower has! As with so many vegetables, it is delicious raw and thus retains the nutrient value.

CAULIFLOWER AND MUSHROOM SOUP

This is a recipe from Brigid Allen, whose wonderful book **'Soup'** has graced my shelves for years. The watercress adds a splash of green which is fun as otherwise the colour can be insipid. Make sure it is properly washed and discard any slimy leaves. You can also use sorrel if you are out foraging.

INGREDIENTS

Large onion
5 tblsp olive oil
1 cauliflower, main stalk discarded and broken in similar-sized florets
10 cloves garlic peeled and chopped
1.5 litres water
1 tsp sea salt
500g button mushrooms, halved
Grated nutmeg
Bunch watercress, washed
2 tblsp shoyu

METHOD

1   Sweat the onion with half the oil in a large pan.
2   Add the cauliflower florets, with half the garlic, and cook very gently with the lid on for 10 minutes. Make sure it doesn't catch on the bottom and burn.
3   Cover with the water and add the sea salt, bring to the boil and simmer for 15 minutes.
4   Stew the mushrooms in the remaining oil and garlic, to allow the liquid to be released.
5   Tip the whole lot into the cauliflower pan with some nutmeg and add the watercress. Cook for a few more minutes and then draw off the heat and cool before liquidising.
6   When serving add a little shoyu, or Worcester sauce.

CAULIFLOWER, SPINACH AND GINGER SOUP

The addition of tomatoes in this soup adds a lovely savoury depth; it also adds to the colour, ideal for slightly over-ripe tomatoes.

INGREDIENTS

2 onions, peeled and chopped
3 tblps vegetable oil
450g cauliflower with core removed and broken into small florets
4 tomatoes, peeled and chopped
4 cloves garlic, peeled
2 cm chunk of fresh ginger root, peeled and chopped
1 tsp sea salt
Freshly ground black pepper
225g spinach leaves, washed thoroughly
1.2 litres water

METHOD

1   Gently sweat the onions in a large heavy-based pan, and then add the cauliflower and stir occasionally to heat through.
2   Add the tomatoes and 3 chopped cloves of garlic, and stir through.
3   Crush the remaining clove of garlic with the ginger and salt in a pestle and mortar and add to the pan; allow to cook very gently for about 15 minutes.
4   Add the spinach and cover with water, bring to the boil and simmer for 20 minutes.
5   Cool a little before liquidising and check for seasoning.

CAULIFLOWER SOUFFLÉ

Using raw cauliflower in this recipe gives it a freshness and texture and the fennel adds a delightful aniseed flavour which combines well.

INGREDIENTS

3 tblsp grated hard cheese (cheddar type)
180g cauliflower florets
1 tblsp finely chopped fennel
115g unsalted butter
Freshly ground black pepper
115g tblsp plain flour
400 mls whole milk
6 large egg yolks
8 large egg whites

METHOD

1   Preheat oven to 200C.
2   Generously butter soufflé dish, then sprinkle with cheese, knocking out excess.
3   Break the cauliflower florets up in a food processor, until quite fine, tip into a bowl and stir in the fennel, 1/4 teaspoon salt, and black pepper to taste.
4   Melt the butter in a heavy based pan over medium heat, stir in the flour, then cook, whisking, until pale golden, about 2 minutes. Add milk a little at a time, whisking constantly until very smooth. Bring sauce to a boil, whisking, then simmer, whisking, until quite thick, about 1 minute. Remove from heat and beat in the yolks, a few grinds black pepper, and 1/2 teaspoon salt. Stir in the cauliflower mixture.
5   Beat whites in a bowl with an electric mixer at high speed until they just hold stiff peaks (they should not look dry). Stir a spoonful of whites into yolk mixture to lighten, then gently fold the mixture into the remaining whites until just combined.
6   Gently spoon into the soufflé dish (leave at least 2cm of space at top) and bake until golden brown and top appears set, 35 to 40 minutes.

The dish is also very pretty with a few seared cauliflower slices. Use the recipe on page 33 but with smaller halved florets. Include the beautiful red scallop roes as well; they need very quick cooking.

Ask your fishmonger to separate the roes from the scallops and remove the little muscle which attaches the scallop to the shell.

SCALLOPS WITH CAULIFLOWER PUREE

Keeping with the spice theme, scallops go very well with cauliflower, but unlike the other puree recipe I offer with cheese, this one keeps the flavours simpler to act as a foil for the sublime texture of the scallops and the spice of curry.

INGREDIENTS

65g unsalted butter
½ large cauliflower, stem removed
    and broken into small,
    even-sized florets
250ml whole milk
¼ tsp sea salt

12 hand-dived scallops
Pinch salt
½ tsp turmeric
½ tsp medium curry powder
Juice of half a lemon
A little olive oil for cooking

METHOD

1 Prepare the puree first. Melt a tsp of the butter in a saucepan, add the cauliflower florets and cook gently for a few minutes, add the salt and milk, bring to a quivering simmer, and cook for about 10 minutes. Make sure the base of the pan does not 'catch' and burn.

2 Strain the cauliflower and put in a food processor with just enough of the cooking liquid to form a smooth puree, set aside and keep warm.

3 Mix the spices together with the salt and roll the scallops in the mixture. Heat a heavy- based pan with a smear of olive oil and quickly sear the scallops for about a minute on each side to give a light brown crust. Cook the roes at the same time and set both aside.

4 If using cauliflower florets, cook them quickly in the same pan, set aside to keep warm.

5 Take the pan off the heat and add the remaining butter and return to the heat. Once it foams up and begins to turn light brown, pour in the lemon juice. Remove from the heat.

6 Place three blobs of puree on each plate and place a scallop on top with the grilled florets and the roes, drizzle the lemon/butter mix over the top; a little colour by way of watercress or rocket adds to the overall look.

CAULIFLOWER PUREE

A rich creamy puree to accompany any roast meat and, if you avoid the crème fraiche at the end, is excellent if you don't want cream or milk. It is also delicious on its own as a main course for a vegetarian. You can add herbs such as thyme, rosemary or fennel as you puree it.

INGREDIENTS

1 head cauliflower, stem removed and head chopped into small florets
100ml chicken or vegetable stock
2 large garlic cloves, peeled
2 tblsp grated Parmesan cheese
½ tsp sea salt, plus more to taste
Freshly ground black pepper
2 tblsp crème fraiche

METHOD

1   Bring the stock to a simmer with the salt and garlic, add the cauliflower and cook very gently until the cauliflower is soft. Make sure the liquid doesn't evaporate.
2   Remove from heat and allow to cool a little, then whizz in a food processor until smooth. Add the cheese and season to taste.
3   Fold in the crème fraiche.

PURPLE CAULIFLOWER HUMMUS

A delightful different dip and the colour is glorious.

INGREDIENTS

1 whole head garlic
5 tblsp olive oil
1 purple cauliflower (about 600g), cut into florets
½ tsp sea salt
3 tblsp lemon juice
Freshly ground black pepper
Lemon wedges, for serving

METHOD

1   Position a rack in the middle of the oven and preheat to 200 C, gas mark 6. Line a baking sheet with greaseproof paper.
2   Peel off most of the papery outer layer from the head of garlic, but leave the head intact. Cut across the very top of the head to expose the cloves. Place the garlic on a sheet of foil and drizzle with 1 tblsp olive oil. Crumple the edges of the foil around the garlic to make a packet for roasting, and set aside.
3   In a medium bowl, combine the cauliflower, salt, and 2 tblsp of the olive oil and toss until the cauliflower is well-coated. Spread the cauliflower on the lined baking sheet without overcrowding, and nestle the garlic packet next to the cauliflower.
4   Roast the vegetables on the middle rack for about 40 minutes — the garlic may take about 10 minutes longer than the cauliflower to roast, so check its doneness (it should be soft and spreadable) when you take the cauliflower out of the oven.
5   Allow to cool a little and then squeeze the garlic into a food processor, add the cauliflower with the remaining oil, salt and lemon juice, and puree to a smooth texture.

SPICED HAKE IN A PAPER BAG WITH CAULIFLOWER RICE AND CHARD

There was a fashion (last century!) to cook fish in paper bags (*en papilotte* as the French would say). It was a good way to keep in moisture and juices, and also, for cooking a kipper, it meant that once you had eaten the fish you could simply wrap the bones up and put them straight in the bin. Then fashions changed; but here is a simple but warming idea for those chill autumn/winter days. I use hake here but you could use any fish with a firm texture.

INGREDIENTS

4 hake fillets (about 750g)
1 tblsp grated fresh ginger
1 tblsp soy sauce
½ cauliflower, core removed
3 spring onions finely chopped

1 tsp turmeric
Handful Swiss chard or beetroot leaves
1 tblsp coconut oil
Juice of 2 limes
Salt and pepper

METHOD

1   Preheat the oven to 180C, gas mark 4.
2   Rub the fish with the ginger and soy sauce, set aside.
3   Create cauliflower 'rice' by blitzing in the food processor to make small chunky bits.
4   Heat a tablespoon of coconut oil in a pan and stir-fry the spring onions for a few minutes until soft. Add the turmeric and the cauliflower 'rice' and cook, stirring just long enough to colour the cauliflower.
5   Cut four pieces of greaseproof paper about 40 cm square and spread each base with a little coconut oil, spread over some chard leaves and the cauliflower. Place the fish fillets on top, season and add a squeeze of lime juice.
6   Wrap up, sealing the edges so the juices won't leak out, and bake for 15 minutes. Serve in the bags; pass a pair of scissors round to cut into them and warn guests that the steam coming out will be hot but enjoy the smell!

CAULIFLOWER FENNEL AND MUSTARD SEEDS

Another curry accompaniment or side dish.

INGREDIENTS

1 large cauliflower; you need about 900g of florets
6 tblsp oil
2 tsp fennel seeds
1 tblsp black mustard seeds
4 cloves finely chopped garlic
¼ tsp turmeric
½ tsp cayenne
1 tsp sea salt
Water from a kettle, freshly boiled

METHOD

1   Cut the cauliflower into small florets of similar size and place in a bowl of cold water for half an hour.
2   Heat the oil in a large frying pan, and stir in the fennel and mustard seeds over a gentle heat.
3   As soon as the mustard seeds start to pop, stir in the garlic – making sure it doesn't burn.
4   Drain the cauliflower, add the remaining spices to the pan, and stir in quickly and then add the cauliflower, salt and a little freshly-boiled water.
5   Stir and cook for about 5 minutes; the cauliflower should still be crisp and the water all evaporated.

Remember to keep the florets the same size so they cook at the same time.

HAKE WITH CAULIFLOWER CURRY

Fish and spices are good bedfellows with cauliflower. The salmon is initially merely browned on both sides not cooked and the final cooking occurs when the fish is added at the very end. The heat of the curry will finish the cooking and keep the fish moist.

INGREDIENTS

4 hake fillets @ 180g each, skin removed
½ tsp ground cumin
½ tsp ground coriander
½ tsp ground turmeric
1 tsp salt
1 onion peeled and chopped
2.5 cm chunk fresh ginger peeled and chopped

2 green chillies roughly chopped
Water
6 tblsp oil
350g cauliflower florets
6 tblsp plain yoghurt
Freshly ground black pepper

METHOD

1   Put the hake in a bowl with ½ tsp each of the cumin and coriander and half the quantity of turmeric, and salt. Mix together and leave for at least an hour.

2   Blend the onion, ginger and chillies together with about 3 tblsp water to form a paste.

3   Heat 5 tblsp of oil in a wide pan and brown the cauliflower florets lightly; set aside in a bowl and season with a little salt and black pepper.

4   In the same pan, brown the hake on both sides and set aside.

5   Add more oil to the pan if necessary, pour in the blended spices, and stir until the mixture browns lightly. Add the remaining spices, stirring them in and then while still stirring, spoon in the yoghurt and combine thoroughly.

6   Add about 400ml water and simmer for a few minutes. Carefully push the cauliflower florets into the mixture spreading them evenly and cook for a few minutes.

7   Push the hake fillets in, adding more water if necessary, to completely cover the fish.

8   Spoon the sauce over the fish and turn off the heat. Leave for a few minutes to allow the hake to cook through before serving.

CAULIFLOWER AND RADISH PICKLE

This is a simple Indian side dish. Mild spices go well with cauliflower and so do vegetables with a mild heat, such as turnip or white radish. It takes a few days to mature but keeps very well.

If you add a few red radishes, it all adds to the pretty colour.

INGREDIENTS

225g cauliflower
225g white radish Daikon
4 tsp black mustard seeds
4 tblsp cold-pressed rape seed oil
2 tsp sea salt
½ tsp ground turmeric
1 tsp cayenne pepper

METHOD

1 Cut the cauliflower into similar-sized florets 3cm across and 4cm long.
2 Peel and cut the radish into 1cm rounds, and if the radish is thick, half or quarter the slices. Grind the mustard seeds in a pestle and mortar.
3 In a large frying pan, heat the oil until very hot and then allow to cool.
4 Mix all the other ingredients thoroughly and then mix with the oil.
5 Place in a suitable sterilised jar or jars and cover; leave in a warm place for a few days to develop, shaking two or three times a day. Check for a fermented flavour; then it is ready.
6 Store in a cool place, but use within a month or two.

PICCALILLI

A true classic of the English culinary canon and is really delicious with cheese and cold meats. I have always liked John Tovey's simple recipes and here is his, except he uses frozen beans, but as I generally make this in the summer I use fresh beans. Don't make the mistake of using the overgrown beans from the garden as they still remain stringy!

INGREDIENTS

1.4 litres malt vinegar
1 large cauliflower, cut into small florets with scant amount of stalk
450g runner beans, cut in fingernail-sized pieces
450g onions, peeled and sliced
2 cloves garlic crushed with salt
1 cucumber, peeled and diced
1 tsp grated nutmeg
450g caster sugar
50g English mustard powder
175g plain flour
2 tsp ground turmeric

METHOD

1   Pour the vinegar into a large pan and bring to the boil.
2   Add the cauliflower, beans, onions and garlic and simmer for 10 minutes.
3   Add the cucumber and sugar and simmer for another 5 minutes; the vegetables should still have a 'crunch'.
4   Blend the mustard with the flour and spices to a smooth paste with a little of the cooking liquid and then whisk it slowly back into the main pan. Stir in to blend well and cook for a further 5 minutes.
5   Allow to cool slightly then place into sterilised jars, cover and store for 3 months in a cool place before using.

CAULIFLOWER FLORETS IN BREADCRUMBS

Making your own breadcrumbs is a very satisfying process, as most of us who eat bread will always have crusts left over.

So instead of buying the over-hyped 'panko' or even worse 'Ruskoline' simply follow this method.

Not only will you have lovely breadcrumbs for this cauliflower dish, but you are not wasting bread and they keep in an air-tight container for ages!

When it comes to cooking the cauliflower, you can either shallow fry in a mixture of oil and a little butter or deep fry. If the former, you will need to turn the vegetable over until crisp and evenly golden.

Briefly 'blitz' any leftover bread in a food processor until it is roughly broken up. Spread over a baking sheet and leave in a warm place overnight. If you have an Aga or other stove, then leave in the plate-warming oven, or place in a cooling oven after you have been cooking. Once the breadcrumbs have dried, return to the food processor and now as they are dry and hard they will process down to a fine, coating crumb.

INGREDIENTS

1 cauliflower	Breadcrumbs as above
2 eggs beaten till smooth	Oil
Salt and pepper	

METHOD

1. Break the cauliflower into small even-sized florets and blanche in boiling salted water for a couple of minutes. Refresh in ice-cold water and drain thoroughly in a colander, shaking a little to remove excess water; dry on kitchen towel.
2. Add a little salt and pepper to the beaten egg and dip the florets in, making sure they are well coated, then roll in the breadcrumbs until evenly coated; shake off any excess crumbs.
3. Place the coated florets on a tray keeping them separate.
5. Fry in your chosen method until crisp and brown.

Delicious with a tomato sauce or any dip you like!

BRAISED CAULIFLOWER

As the florets cook in their own juices in this dish, it is important that they are all the same size and the pan is large enough so they can all fit on one layer.

INGREDIENTS

A few saffron strands
1 tblsp raisins
2 tblsp olive oil
1 cauliflower, broken into even-sized florets
2 tblsp flaked almonds
Clove garlic, crushed
½ tsp smoked paprika
Salt and pepper
Chopped flat parsley
1 tsp red wine vinegar

METHOD

1   Soak the saffron with the raisins in enough boiling water to just cover the raisins.
2   Heat the oil in a large sauté pan and add the cauliflower and almonds. Cook, stirring gently until browned, add the garlic and stir for a few more moments.
3   Strain in the saffron water from the raisins, add the paprika, cover and simmer gently for 10 minutes until the cauliflower is just cooked. Discard the saffron.
4   Finish with the raisins, parsley and vinegar, and season with salt and pepper.

CAULIFLOWER AND CHICKPEA CURRY

I use a medium curry powder as the base for this, thus allowing the other spices to come through the basic warmth. As with most curries, it improves with keeping a day or two.

INGREDIENTS

1 cauliflower, cut into medium florets
2 tblsp oil
3 onions peeled and chopped
4 cloves garlic, peeled and chopped
2 tsp grated fresh ginger
4 tsp curry powder
2 star anise
400g tin chopped tomatoes
400g tin chickpeas, drained
2 tsp garam masala
Chopped fresh coriander
Salt and pepper

METHOD

1   Put the cauliflower into a pan and cover with cold water, add salt and bring to the boil, and after a minute remove from the heat and drain, leave in the pan.
2   In a second pan, heat the oil and cook the onions and ginger for a few minutes to soften.
3   Stir in the garlic, curry powder and star anise; cook for a further 5 minutes.
4   Tip in the tomatoes and the chickpeas and stir in thoroughly.
5   Add the cauliflower and enough cooking water to half fill the tomato can, stir well and cook until the cauliflower is just tender.
6   Stir in the garam masala, serve with the coriander sprinkled over.

CAULIFLOWER PAKORA

A versatile little dish, either a first course or a canapé or as part of a selection of spiced dishes , and the raita (flavoured yoghurt) can be used as is, or adapted, but do make sure you use a really good full-fat rich yoghurt base. Bere meal is an old variety of barley grown on Orkney but gram flour or rye will do instead.

INGREDIENTS

1 cauliflower
150g beremeal
½ tsp baking powder
2 tsp ground cumin
2 tsp ground coriander
½ tsp ground turmeric
About 175ml cold water
Paprika (optional)

Raita
6 tblsp full-fat plain yoghurt
Handful chopped mint
2 tsp tamarind paste
Salt and pepper

METHOD

1   Mix the ingredients for the raita together and set aside.
2   Cut the cauliflower into small, similar-sized florets cutting away excess stalk.
3   Sieve the beremeal and spices into a bowl and whisk in the water to achieve a smooth, thick batter. You may need a little more water, but the batter should lightly but thoroughly coat the cauliflower.
4   Heat the oil in a suitable pan; you are deep frying so lots of room!
5   Dip the florets into the batter, drain a little and drop about 5 or 6 florets at a time into the hot oil. Cook for a few minutes until crisp and light brown.
6   Drain on kitchen paper, dust with paprika (optional) and serve with the raita.

ROASTED CAULIFLOWER WITH LEMON AND PAPRIKA

At once simple, but the lemon juice and smoked paprika really show off the lovely flavours of the cauliflower.

INGREDIENTS

1 medium cauliflower
2 lemons
3 tblsp olive oil
½ tsp smoked paprika
Coarse sea salt

METHOD

1   Preheat the oven to 220C, gas mark 8
2   Cut the cauliflower into medium even-sized florets and wash, leaving some water adhering.
3   Mix in a bowl with the oil, the juice from one lemon, paprika and a little salt and pepper.
4   Place in a roasting tray with the remaining lemon, cut into 6 segments, and roast for about half an hour until the edges are just browning.
5   Squeeze over the juice from the cooked lemons and serve with a scattering of sea salt.

CAULIFLOWER CAKE

Ottolenghi's take on cauliflower cheese! This recipe is from 'Plenty More' and is fun to do as it is unusual. But do not be led into thinking this is like a carrot cake to serve as a pudding! It is quite definitely savoury!

INGREDIENTS

About 450g cauliflower florets
2 red onions, peeled
75ml olive oil
1 tsp finely chopped thyme or lemon thyme
7 eggs
120g plain flour
1½ tsp baking powder
½ tsp turmeric
150g coarsely grated hard cheese
Melted butter
2 tsp mixture of sesame seeds and poppy seeds

METHOD

1   Cook the cauliflower florets in a pan of boiling salted water for about 10 minutes. Drain and set aside to dry completely.
2   Cut the onions into 5 thin rings, set aside, then roughly chop the rest and cook in the oil with the chopped thyme, until soft.
3   In a large bowl, whisk the eggs and add the flour, baking powder, turmeric, cheese and cooked onions; fold in the cooked cauliflower and season.
4   Set the oven to 200C, gas mark 6.
5   Line a 24cm drop-based tin with cling film and spoon the mixture in. Spread the sliced onions over the top and brush with melted butter; finally sprinkle with the seed mix.
6   Bake for 45 minutes until golden brown and set.

Serve warm

CAULIFLOWER BALLS

This recipe is ideal for left-over cauliflower or one which is not looking great, as you cook it and process into very small pieces. The seasoning given here is simple but feel free to experiment with stronger spices or grated lemon zest. You can also serve them with different dips such as a tomato sauce or a raita.

INGREDIENTS

1 cauliflower, broken into even-sized florets
Salt and pepper
25g mild Anster cheese grated
2 slices white bread, soaked in milk and squeezed dry
Grated nutmeg
1 large egg
100g breadcrumbs (see 'Florets in Breadcrumbs', p31)
Oil for deep frying

METHOD

1   Cook the florets in boiling salted water until soft – 8 minutes or so.
2   Drain and use a food processor to break into small pieces and leave to cool.
3   Mix in the cheese and soaked bread and season with salt, pepper and nutmeg.
4   Form into small balls about 2.5cm wide.
5   Roll in egg wash and breadcrumbs (see 'Florets in Breadcrumbs', p31).
6   Deep fry until crisp and golden.

CAULIFLOWER AND MACKEREL WITH A LIGHT BATTER

If you use fresh yeast, the batter will become frothy quickly but if you only have dried yeast then make the batter as the recipe, but allow it to sit for 15 minutes before using to allow the yeast to start to become active. I have used mackerel here but you can use any oily fish, such as herring or even salmon.

INGREDIENTS

1 cauliflower cut into florets
250g plain flour
150ml tepid water
1 large egg beaten
10g fresh yeast
1 mackerel, filleted and cut into strips
Oil for frying
Smoked paprika

METHOD

1   Cook the cauliflower in boiling salted water for 5 minutes, drain and dry.
2   Combine the flour, water, egg and yeast to make the batter; it needs to be quite liquid, and starting to froth.
3   Coat the cauliflower florets thoroughly in the batter and deep fry until crisp and golden.
4   Repeat with the mackerel and serve with a dusting of smoked paprika and 'Trotter's Hot Pepper Jelly'.

CAULIFLOWER SALAD WITH OLIVES

This idea is good with baby cauliflower; one of the colourful ones or the beautiful pale green romanesco.

Anchovies are traditional in it but for a more northern hemisphere taste, try using smoked herring. Don't use olives in brine; I prefer the ones in a dry Mediterranean herb marinade.

INGREDIENTS

1 head of cauliflower or romanesco
1 tblsp olive oil
1 tsp white wine vinegar
Freshly ground black pepper
1 tsp 'Trotter's Hot Pepper' dipping sauce
100g anchovy fillets in oil, chopped
16 pitted black olives
2 spring onions chopped
2 hard boiled eggs chopped
Clove garlic, finely chopped
Chopped flat parsley

METHOD

1   Break the cauliflower into florets and cook in boiling salted water for two minutes, drain and leave to cool.
2   Make a dressing with the olive oil, vinegar, pepper, dipping sauce and anchovies.
3   Mix the cauliflower with the dressing and add the spring onions and olives. Place in a serving bowl and sprinkle over with the chopped egg, parsley and garlic.

CAULIFLOWER WITH SAFFRON AND PINE NUTS

A lovely Sicilian dish using saffron to infuse flavour; with texture and sweetness from pine nuts and raisins. I like to use purple cauliflower or romanesco, which really adds colour. If you make the florets quite small, the dish makes a good sauce for pasta as well as simply a side dish.

INGREDIENTS

1 cauliflower
3 tblsp pine nuts
3 tblsp olive oil
1 large onion thinly sliced
½ tsp strands saffron, infused in 4 tblsp boiling water
75g raisins, rinsed in warm water
Salt and pepper

METHOD

1 Break the cauliflower into florets, retaining the small green leaves, and blanche in boiling salted water for a minute, drain and set aside.
2 Dry-roast the pine nuts in a large pan until lightly browned, set aside, and wipe out the pan.
3 Heat the oil in the pan and stir in the onion with a little salt, reduce heat and stirring regularly cook for about 15 minutes until golden. Drain the oil, set the onions aside and wipe the pan.
4 Return the oil to the pan and over a high heat fry the cauliflower and the leaves for a few minutes until it colours lightly. Stir in the onions and the pine nuts, raisins and the saffron-infused water; cook until the water has pretty much evaporated mixing everything thoroughly, season and serve.

CAULIFLOWER PARFAIT WITH CAVIAR

This is a real departure for me to use such an extravagant ingredient as caviar but one of my favourite cook books is the 'Dean and Deluca' cookbook and they really rate the combination, so here goes for a bit of indulgence!

(Serves 8 very small portions)

INGREDIENTS

175g raw cauliflower florets
1 medium, waxy potato peeled and cut into chunks
Freshly ground black pepper
Sea salt
50ml double cream
175g caviar (the best you can afford!!). http://www.kingsfinefood.co.uk/ do an excellent caviar and mail order

METHOD

1   Cook the potato and cauliflower together in a pan of boiling salted water for about 20 minutes until thoroughly cooked, drain, and blitz in a food processor. ('D and D' pass it though a fine cloth! But I think this is unnecessary)

2   Return the puree to the pan and dry it out over a low heat for a few minutes; stir occasionally to prevent it burning. Season quite heavily as it will be served cold and cold food needs more seasoning. Chill until very cold.

3   Whip the cream until light and just holding, and gently fold it into the cauliflower mixture. Chill again until very cold.

4   To serve take small egg cups or glasses and place a small amount of caviar in the base, then top up with the cauliflower mixture and then finish with a blob of caviar on the top. Chill and serve very cold.

CAULIFLOWER FRITTERS

A lovely fresh but lightly spiced Lebanese Mezze dish which I was given in Beirut a few years ago.

INGREDIENTS

1 small cauliflower
120g plain flour
3 tblsp chopped flat leaf parsley
Clove of garlic, crushed
2 shallots finely chopped
4 eggs
1½ tsp ground cumin
1 tsp ground coriander
½ tsp turmeric
Salt and freshly ground black pepper
Oil for frying

METHOD

1   Cut the cauliflower into florets and cook in boiling salted water for 15 minutes then drain.
2   Put the flour, parsley, garlic, shallots, eggs and spices into a bowl and whisk to form a batter. Break up the warm florets and mix into the batter, season with salt and pepper.
3   Deep fry spoonfuls in hot oil for 3 – 4 minutes and drain on kitchen paper.

LAMBS' KIDNEYS WITH CAULIFLOWER AND SPRING ONIONS

An unusual Chinese dish, but the combination of flavours and textures is surprisingly satisfying. This could be served as part of a series of small dishes.

INGREDIENTS

4 lamb kidneys
2 tblsp dry sherry
1 cauliflower
Salt
2 tblsp oil
4 spring onions
1 tsp cornflour
1 tblsp soy sauce
2 tblsp water
1 tsp brown sugar

METHOD

1   Cut the kidneys in half and core them, then cut in a criss-cross and marinate in the sherry for 15 minutes.
2   Break the cauliflower into florets and cook in boiling salted water for a few minutes, drain and allow to dry.
3   Drain the kidneys and reserve the sherry, dab dry with kitchen paper.
4   Heat the oil in a pan until very hot and quickly brown the kidneys, add the spring onions and cauliflower and stir together for a few minutes.
5   Mix the remaining ingredients together with the reserved sherry, and a little salt. Pour into the pan and mix together. Cook for a few more minutes until thickened and coated, add some chopped coriander for colour, if you feel it needs it!

MASHED POTATOES WITH CAULIFLOWER AND CUMIN

A very versatile 'side'; this will accompany many dishes from fish to lamb or is delicious with a few roast vegetables and a sprinkling of toasted seeds.

INGREDIENTS

1.5 kg potatoes, peeled and quartered
1 cauliflower, broken into florets
1 tblsp cumin seeds
225ml milk
Salt and pepper
2 tblsp olive oil
Chopped chives

METHOD

1   Place the potatoes in a large pan with salted cold water, (leaving room to add the cauliflower later) and bring to the boil and simmer for 15 minutes. Add the cauliflower and cook until both are soft. Drain through a colander and dry thoroughly.

2   Heat the milk and dry roast the cumin seeds in a pan and add to the warm milk.

3   Mash the vegetables thoroughly and then stir in the heated milk with the cumin seeds; season and serve liberally; drizzled with the olive oil and chopped chives.

ROAST CAULIFLOWER WITH RED ONIONS AND ROSEMARY

A simple and colourful mixture to go with a roast, in particular roast lamb.

INGREDIENTS

2 cauliflowers broken into quite large florets
3 red onions peeled and cut into 8 wedges each
4 cloves garlic crushed
2 tblsp cold-pressed rape seed oil
1 tblsp chopped fresh rosemary
Salt and pepper

METHOD

1   Set the oven to 230C, gas mark 8
2   In a bowl, mix the vegetables to coat with the garlic and oil, then place in a roasting tray and cook, turning occasionally until tender and browned.
3   Throw in the rosemary and season, serve.

CREME DUBARRY

A correspondence on 'Facebook' with cooks I admire, flagged up a mutual respect for the one-time owners of 'La Potiniere', Gullane, David and Hilary Brown, from whose book, 'La Potiniere and Friends', this recipe is taken as my homage to them – the consummate restaurateurs. I should call it 'Goat's head soup'!

INGREDIENTS

50g unsalted butter
1 large white onion peeled and finely sliced
Clove garlic, peeled and crushed
1 tsp mustard powder
150ml dry sherry
Medium cauliflower broken into florets
Double cream
Chopped parsley or dill

METHOD

1   Melt the butter in a medium pan, soften and lightly colour the sliced onions.
2   Add the garlic, mustard, half the sherry and cauliflower, cover and cook gently for 5 minutes.
3   Add 600ml water and simmer until cauliflower is cooked, about 50 minutes.
4   Liquidise and then sieve for a really smooth texture, add the remaining sherry and season.
5   Serve with a little whipped cream and chopped herbs.

BENGALI FISH CURRY WITH CAULIFLOWER AND POTATO

This recipe is adapted from my friend Simon Parkes's book on Calcutta.

It is very good with freshwater fish, such as pike or perch, but a firm white-fleshed sea fish is fine.

INGREDIENTS

450g pike fillets, cut into about 8 pieces
Salt
2 tsp turmeric
1 tsp cumin seeds
1 tsp mustard seeds
3cm piece of fresh ginger, peeled and chopped
1 large onion peeled and chopped

4 tblsp oil
½ tsp onion seeds
1 tsp chilli powder
2 tsp ground coriander
1 large potato cut into wedges
1 small cauliflower, cut into florets
Fresh chopped coriander

METHOD

1 Rub the fish fillets with a little salt and 1 tsp turmeric.
2 Soak the mustard seeds and cumin with the remaining turmeric in 4 tblsp warm water for 10 minutes and then puree in a blender with the ginger and onion, adding more water to create a very smooth paste.
3 Heat a large pan or wok with a little oil and fry the fish until crisp, set aside.
4 Add a little more oil and fry the onion seeds, briefly, and then pour in the onion puree, the remaining turmeric and chilli.
5 Add the potato wedges and reduce the heat, cook for a few minutes, then add the cauliflower and a little more water, simmer for another 10 minutes. Turn off the heat and gently place the fish pieces into the mixture, leave for a few minutes to heat through and serve taking care not to break up the fish pieces.

Serve with rice and the chopped coriander.

CAULIFLOWER CHEESE WITH HAM AND TOMATOES

Well this had to be in there didn't it! I have taken a leaf out of Dorothy Hartley and cooked this whole but do break it up and cook in florets if you prefer.

INGREDIENTS

1 whole cauliflower with the inner leaves still attached
500ml milk
Bay leaf
Parsley stalks
100g butter
50g flour
2 tsp mustard powder
300g grated cheddar cheese
Slices of ham
3 tomatoes sliced

METHOD

1   Make some deep cuts upwards from the base to allow the cauliflower to cook quickly in boiling salted water for about 10 minutes. Lift out and drain, then sit on a piece of toast to really dry out.
2   Make the cheese sauce; heat the milk in a pan with a bay leaf and some parsley stalks and leave to infuse.
3   Set the oven to 220C, gas mark 7.
4   Melt the butter in a pan and stir in the flour and mustard powder. Strain the hot milk through a sieve into the pan, stirring all the time to form a smooth sauce, discard the herbs.
5   Sprinkle in the cheese and stir until it melts.
6   Place the cauliflower in an oven-proof dish. Place a few slices of ham and tomato on top; cover in the sauce and bake in the oven until lightly browned.

GRILLED SLICE OF CAULIFLOWER

Very simple to do and makes a great base to put things on with a sauce, such as roast peppers or some grilled fish, or try dusting with a favourite spice before cooking. You may need a couple of cauliflowers as the florets can fall off the slices, so use these in another recipe.

INGREDIENTS

Whole cauliflower
Olive oil
Salt and pepper

METHOD

1   Place the cauliflower, base down, on a chopping board and using a large knife carefully cut slices about 2 cm thick straight down; allow a slice per person.
2   Bathe in olive oil and season with salt and pepper, adding your own spices as you like.
3   Heat a griddle pan or use a barbecue and place the slices onto the hot metal; leave for a few minutes to allow the markings to form.
4   You can turn the slices at 90 degrees to give the criss-cross look or just turn over, but cooking time will be about 3 minutes on each side to give a crisp texture, and a good colour.

BIOGRAPHIES

CAROLINE TROTTER is a freelance photographer and works across a wide variety of subjects. Weddings are her main area of work but she also does portraits, both human and animal – horses, dogs etc. Caroline covers events for associations such as Fife Chamber of Commerce and provides business portraits for websites and marketing purposes, and food photography for websites and restaurants. She also runs photography courses from home. She is a qualified member of the Master Photographers Association and the Society of Wedding and Portrait photographers.

www.carolinetrotter.co.uk

CHRISTOPHER TROTTER is Fife's Food Ambassador, an honorary title bestowed on him for his work promoting food from Fife. He is also a freelance chef, cookery writer and food commentator, appearing on programmes such as BBC Radio Scotland's *Kitchen Café* and *Kitchen Garden*. He is a committee member of The Guild of Food Writers and is a sought-after speaker at events and after dinner. As a consultant, he has worked with agencies as diverse as Argyll and the Island's Enterprise and The National Trust for Scotland. Christopher also provides cookery classes and food tours and he is passionate about fresh produce in its season.

www.fifefoodambassador.co.uk

They have two children and two dogs and live in rural Fife.

CHRISTOPHER TROTTER

A bit more about me! This is my fifth book in my vegetable series, so if you like this one do look out for the others, *Beetroot ,Courgette, Kale* and *Carrot* you can get them from my website (Christophertrotter.co.uk). I also have other cook books available, have a look on line (*The Whole Hog, The Whole Cow* and various on Scottish cooking and gastronomy).

Here are a few other things that I do which may be of interest to you dear reader:

COOKING CLASSES
These are all bespoke, based on whatever you want to do.

An ideal present for a couple or a family. I can travel! Or why not come to beautiful Fife (http://www.welcometofife.com/) for a holiday and come to my kitchen.

A few ideas . . . Vegetables, shellfish, game, fish, fruit, Scottish classics, a seasonal menu . . .

FOOD TOURS
These can be a simple tour round Fife, which is my region in Scotland, showing you where food is grown and produced, we can visit cheesemakers, growers, farmers etc. see where the lobster and shellfish are landed and enjoy a simple meal of fresh seasonal produce. Or I can organise a larger group to do a food based tour over any part of Scotland from Galloway to Orkney and all in between!

PRESENTATIONS AND LECTURES
I can come and speak to your company, club or association on subjects as diverse as " The history of Scotland through kale!" or "Stories from the Savoy and other kitchens"

Or if you have any other food based ideas why not get in touch!

07739049639

ct@christophertrotter.co.uk

christophertrotter.co.uk

ACKNOWLEDGEMENTS AND THANKS

This is the fifth book in my series of 'Little Vegetable' books and once again I have so enjoyed discovering more about cauliflower. My main source of information comes from the 'Riverford Farm Cook Book', a worthy winner of the Guild of Food Writers cookbook of the year. So my thanks for inspiration goes to Guy Watson and of course June Baxter who continues to give such pleasure each year at the Guild awards ceremony where she provides superb food. Otherwise my go-to cooks and chefs for inspiration tend to be the same as in previous books. Whether still alive or not Roger Verge and Michel Guerard opened my eyes to possibilities, and then my contemporary heroes and those whose ideas appear in these pages, Sybil Kapoor, Simon Parkes, John Tovey, Raymond Blanc, Madhur Jaffrey and many more.

LOCH LEVEN'S LARDER

Loch Leven's Larder is located on our farm, Channel of Pittendreich, a 700 acre vegetable farm blessed with the perfect conditions for vegetable farming: high rainfall, a south-facing aspect, and cool summer temperatures.

We are delighted to sponsor this book – like us, Christopher is a passionate advocate for vegetables, as this inspiring series demonstrates, and for seasonal food sourced locally. We grow leeks, sweetheart cabbage, savoy, carrots, broccoli, Brussel sprouts, kohlrabi, beetroot, curly kale, courgettes, cavolo nero, hispi cabbage, romanesco, pumpkins, parsnips, turnips, oats, wheat and of course, cauliflowers.

Loch Leven's Larder opened in 2005 and today, the field to fork concept remains central to everything we do. We've grown into a multi award-winning dining and retail destination but we're proud of the simple things too – our flavourful vegetables, our honest approach to food production and opening up our fields so that people can walk alongside our crops as they travel along Loch Leven's Heritage Trail.

Situated on the border of Perthshire and Fife, both areas with a rich heritage of quality food and drink, we source as much of our produce from these counties as possible, before looking to the rest of Scotland and further afield to meet our needs. These quality goods are sold in our shop and also used by our kitchen with our own produce to create delicious seasonal meals and treats to sell in our well-stocked deli.

We hope you'll come and visit us soon, stop for a bite to eat, visit our deli, and perhaps pick up a cauliflower and try one of Christopher's recipes.

DIRECTIONS

Loch Leven's Larder is easily accessible from Edinburgh, Perth and Dundee, just minutes from the M90. Situated on the North side of Loch Leven we can be approached from the East on the A911 from Scotlandwell; from the West on the B911 from Milnathort or Kinross; and from the North on the B916 from the main St. Andrews to Stirling (A91) road.

To book a table or for general enquiries, please call us on 01592 841000 or visit www.lochlevenslarder.com

NOTES

NOTES